Reinforced Learning in Content-Based Recommender Systems

Table of Contents

1. Introduction 1

2. Introduction to Reinforced Learning 2

   2.1. Understanding the Basics 2

   2.2. Duel of Exploration and Exploitation 3

   2.3. Markov Decision Processes 3

   2.4. Q-Learning and Policy Iteration 4

   2.5. Reinforcement Learning in Modern Applications 4

3. The Anatomy of Content-Based Recommender Systems 6

   3.1. Understanding Content-Based Recommender Systems 6

   3.2. How CBRS Work: Under the hood 7

   3.3. The Role of Machine Learning in CBRS 7

   3.4. Evaluating the Effectiveness of CBRS 8

   3.5. Addressing Challenges and Road Ahead 8

4. Evolution of Recommender Systems: A Historical Perspective . . . 10

   4.1. The Rise of Collaborative Filtering 10

   4.2. The Magic of Hybrid Systems 11

   4.3. The Era of Deep Learning 11

   4.4. The Future of Recommender Systems 12

5. Synergy between Reinforced Learning and Recommender
Systems 13

   5.1. Foundations of Reinforced Learning 13

   5.2. RL in the Context of Recommender Systems 14

   5.3. Combining RL with Traditional Methods 14

   5.4. Case Study: RL-Driven Recommendation at Youtube 15

   5.5. Overcoming the Cold Start Problem with RL 15

   5.6. Balancing Exploration and Exploitation 15

6. Data Requirements: The Fuel of Reinforced Learning 17

   6.1. Understanding Data in Reinforced Learning 17

6.2. Quality and Quantity: The Balancing Act 17

6.3. Diversity: Encouraging Exploration 18

6.4. Utility: Meaningful Data for Valuable Interactions 19

6.5. Real World Data Challenges 19

6.6. Reinforced Learning in Content-Based Recommender
Systems 19

7. The Mechanics of Content Personalization 21

7.1. Reinforcement Learning-Based Personalization 21

7.2. The role of Bandit Algorithms 22

7.3. Data Selection and Feature Extraction 22

7.4. Challenges in Implementing RL-based Personalization ... 23

7.5. The Future of Personalization 23

8. Case Studies: Successful Applications of Reinforced Learning ... 25

8.1. Ghostly Assistants: Reinforcement Learning in Gaming ... 25

8.2. Street-Smart Intelligence: Reinforcement Learning in
Autonomous Vehicles 25

8.3. Engaging Grooves: Reinforcement Learning in Music
Recommendation 26

8.4. Trading Profits: Reinforcement Learning in Financial
Systems 26

8.5. Personalized Entertainments: Reinforcement Learning in
Streaming Services 27

8.6. Enhanced Cybersecurity: Reinforcement Learning in
Defensive Systems 27

9. Challenges and Ethical Considerations in Utilizing Reinforced
Learning 28

9.1. Overcoming the Challenges in the Application of RL ... 28

9.2. Ethical Quandaries in RL 29

9.3. Future Directions 30

10. The Future: Emerging Trends and Opportunities 31

10.1. Reinforcing E-Commerce 31

10.2. Entertainment and Streaming Platforms 32

10.3. Transcending into the Healthcare Sphere 32

10.4. Customer Service Enhanced with AI 33

10.5. Progress and Prospects 33

11. Final Thoughts: The Road Ahead for Reinforced Learning in
Recommender Systems 34

11.1. The Potential of RL Based Recommender Systems 34

11.2. Tackling Technical Challenges 35

11.3. Next-Gen RL Algorithms and Models 35

11.4. A Shift Towards User-Centric Approach 36

11.5. Conclusion 36

Chapter 1. Introduction

In this Special Report, we dive deep into the innovative world of machine learning, more precisely, Reinforced Learning and its groundbreaking applications in Content-Based Recommender Systems. While the subject is indeed technical, it holds a captivating promise of shaping our digital interactions in ways that feel almost intuitive. The report cautiously uncovers the complexity behind these advanced processes without overwhelming or intimidating you with jargon. Instead, it provides a clear, comprehensive understanding of how these technologies work, their potential, and their growing influence on our day-to-day lives. Designed for both a novice and an expert eye, this report is an exploration of the fascinating dance between artificial intelligence and personalized content delivery. Consider this an invitation to delve into the compelling intersection of machine learning and digital content, a journey that is as enlightening as it is relevant in today's connected world.

Chapter 2. Introduction to Reinforced Learning

In the past decade or so, we have been fascinated and sometimes surprised by the rapid advancement of technologies that, until recently, appeared to be the exclusive realm of science fiction. Machine learning, a vital wing of artificial intelligence (AI), has significantly contributed to fueling this sense of wonder. At the heart of many of these technologies, lies Reinforcement Learning (RL), an intricate yet extraordinarily potent subset of machine learning that has found profound applications across myriad of fields.

2.1. Understanding the Basics

As a primer, Reinforcement Learning involves an agent that learns to make decisions by executing certain actions in an environment, to reach a specific goal. This process, at a fundamental level, mirrors the way humans and animals learn. Drawing analogies from incentives or discouragements we experience, RL involves reward (positive reinforcement) or penalty (negative reinforcement) as a principle based on the agent's actions. The agent tries to maximize the cumulative rewards over time, adapting its strategy or 'policy' with every interaction. This trial-and-error learning, continuously fine-tuning actions based on outcomes, lies at the core of RL.

Framing the RL process in formal terms, we encounter key components, namely agents and environments, actions, states, and rewards. The agent interacts with the environment by actions resulting in changes to the environment or the agent's state within it. Each action, based on the prevailing state, yields a reward (which could be positive, negative, or zero) and moves the agent to a new state.

2.2. Duel of Exploration and Exploitation

In the world of RL, there is a constant struggle between two competing requirements: exploration and exploitation. Here, exploration refers to the agent's attempt to gather new knowledge by trying different actions and gauging their impact. Conversely, exploitation represents the use of known knowledge to maximize the reward. Striking the right balance between these two strategies is vital and poses a challenging conundrum known as the exploration-exploitation dilemma. How much to explore and when to exploit are intricate questions that RL has to address to be efficient.

2.3. Markov Decision Processes

Central to understanding RL is the concept of Markov Decision Processes (MDPs), which provide a mathematical framework to model decision making in situations where outcomes are partly random and partly determined by the actions of an agent. In MDPs, an entity's future state depends solely on the current state and action, not on the sequence of events that led to the current state. This principle is known as the Markov property.

MDPs describe the environment for RL. Every MDP is defined by a tuple comprising states (S), actions (A), model (T), and reward ®.

- 'S' is the set of states that an agent can be in, within the environment. For a game of chess, for instance, every unique arrangement of pieces on the board would constitute a state.

- 'A' is the set of all possible actions available to the agent. For a chess-playing agent, any legal move would be an action.

- 'T' is the transition model that describes the probability of landing in a state 's1', upon performing action 'a' in state 's'.

- 'R' is the reward function that gives the agent a certain numerical reward for an action taken in a particular state leading to a new state.

Once defined, an agent operates within this model, learning the optimal policy (strategy) to maximize its cumulative reward over time.

2.4. Q-Learning and Policy Iteration

To solve the MDP and find the optimal policy, various techniques have been advanced, two of which are Q-learning and Policy Iteration.

Q-learning is an off-policy RL algorithm that seeks to find the optimal policy by learning the value of actions, known as Q-values. These values are learned via interactions with the environment and updated iteratively using the Bellman Equation.

In contrast, Policy Iteration is an in-policy method that involves repeatedly improving and evaluating a policy until it converges on the optimal solution. This technique typically applies value iteration to calculate the value function for a given policy and then updates the policy based on the calculated values.

2.5. Reinforcement Learning in Modern Applications

RL is being utilized in diverse applications ranging from gaming and robotics to finance, healthcare, and content recommendation systems. In games and robotics, RL helps machines surpass human-level performances, learning from scratch to make strategically sound decisions. Meanwhile, sectors like healthcare benefit from RL optimizing treatment policies and personalized treatment designs. Financial trading uses RL for portfolio management and algorithmic trading systems.

A very prominent application that touches almost everybody's lives is content-based recommendation systems. Today's digital space is flooded with content from various sources, and RL-based algorithms help tailor this content to individual users' preferences, learning from their past interactions and engagement. Through an RL framework, recommendation systems can recommend articles, videos, products, and news that cater to your interests, making the internet's vastness more manageable and personal.

As we advance further into this report, we will unravel how Reinforcement Learning fuels these personal recommendation systems, transforming our digital landscape into an engaging, personalized experience. The journey awaits.

Chapter 3. The Anatomy of Content-Based Recommender Systems

A compelling dance between artificial intelligence and personalized content delivery occurs within the sphere of content-based recommender systems (CBRS). To truly appreciate the intricacies of this relationship, one must first understand the core components and operating ideologies behind it.

3.1. Understanding Content-Based Recommender Systems

CBRS are an integral tool for many consumer-facing services. They use detailed information about each item in a database and profile user interactions to suggest content that is rendered the most relevant. This approach underpins systems ranging from music and movie suggestions on Spotify or Netflix to product recommendations on ecommerce platforms like Amazon.

The term "content-based" arises from the system's ability to create recommendations based on the intrinsic characteristics of items. Rather than relying solely on user-user interactions, CBRS use item-item relationships, enhancing the precision of the recommendations. The content analysed is broad, spanning from text data like titles, descriptions, and categories, to numerical data like prices, ratings, and other characteristics.

To link users with the most suitable content, the system creates a profile for each user based on their previous interactions. This insightful profile shapes the line of recommendations, attempting to mimic the user's behavior and tastes.

3.2. How CBRS Work: Under the hood

Content-based recommender systems operate in three main stages to create user-focused recommendations:

1. Content Representation: The system needs to understand the items in its database before it can match them with users. Each item is represented as a 'feature vector', a set of characteristics that accurately conveys its nature. For example, a book's feature vector might include the genre, author, language, publication year, and so forth.

2. User Profile Construction: This is the process of learning the user's tastes. Each interaction a user has with an item, such as a rating, or even the duration of interaction, contributes to building a comprehensive user profile. The system then relates the user's profile feature vector with the item's feature vector.

3. Recommendation: Using sophisticated algorithms and techniques such as cosine similarity or machine learning models, the system will generate a list of potential item matches for the user. These items align with the user's feature vector, which is parsed consistently to guarantee accurate recommendations.

3.3. The Role of Machine Learning in CBRS

Reinforced Learning, a component of Machine Learning, has brought commendable enhancement to CBRS. This technology mimics the human learning process - learning by trial and error or reward and punishment, enabling the system to make more intuitive recommendations.

An RL-based Recommender System uses interactions with the user as 'feedback' to optimise recommendations. A positive interaction (a reward, such as a high rating for a product) steers the system towards similar recommendations, while a negative interaction (a punishment, such as a low rating or non-engagement) makes the system less likely to recommend similar products.

With every interaction, the system evaluates and adjusts its model, continually aiming to optimise its recommendations. This 'learning' process sets RL apart, providing an almost sentient ability to adapt to the growing and changing needs of users.

3.4. Evaluating the Effectiveness of CBRS

To assess the performance of a content-based recommender system, different metrics are applied depending on the desired outcomes. These include Precision, Recall, F1 Score, RMSE (Root Mean Squared Error), and others. Precision looks at the relevancy of recommendations, while Recall considers the total amount of relevant products that should have been recommended. F1 Score, on the other hand, provides the harmonic mean of Precision and Recall, giving a balanced perspective. RMSE looks at prediction accuracy - essentially, how far off were the predictions from actual ratings.

Apart from these quantitative measures, qualitative measures such as user surveys could also be used to gauge users' satisfaction and their perception towards the recommendations they are getting.

3.5. Addressing Challenges and Road Ahead

Despite its efficiencies, CBRS are not without challenges. A major concern is that they tend to limit their recommendations to items similar to those the user has already interacted with, leading to a sort of "filter bubble" that can stifle discovery of diverse content.

Another challenge is the 'cold start' problem – when a new user or item is added to the system, the lack of previous interaction history hinders generating accurate recommendations. Similar challenges arise for existing users with changes in behavior patterns over time.

A potential solution to these issues comes with the blending of content-based recommender systems with other recommendation models, like collaborative filtering and hybrid models. By amalgamating the strengths of different models, more robust, relevant, and diverse recommendations can be offered.

Machine Learning, especially Reinforced Learning, is still evolving and continues to open new frontiers in content-based recommender systems. By harmonizing user-content relevance with user freedom of choice, the landscape of personalized digital experiences can become more intuitive and immersive than ever before.

This arduous journey of investigating the intricacies of the content-based recommender systems provides an impressive standpoint on the depth and breadth of possibilities before us. The unraveling of how this complex system learns, optimises, and continuously evolves creates a more substantial appreciation of how intertwined our lives have become with technology, allowing for some truly exciting implications for the future.

Chapter 4. Evolution of Recommender Systems: A Historical Perspective

To begin, one must understand the humble yet instrumental beginnings of recommender systems. Originating from the field of information retrieval and information filtering, recommender systems in the simplest terms are tools designed to predict user preferences. The initial attention towards developing such systems can be traced back to the late 1970s and 1980s, though the term 'recommender system' did not come into vogue until the late 1990s.

The early stage systems developed were largely content-based, focusing on item attributes to make recommendations. These primitive systems were heavily dependent on capturing explicit user preferences, usually through the tedious task of rating items or making selections. However, as technology advanced and the Internet exploded into prominence, the ways in which these systems functioned began to change.

4.1. The Rise of Collaborative Filtering

Perhaps one of the most significant shifts in the evolution of recommender systems is the development of collaborative filtering (CF) techniques in the mid-1990s. The term 'collaborative filtering' first emerged from a report by Goldberg et al. (1992), detailing the GroupLens system, an automated, collaborative filtering based newsgroup filtering system.

The fundamental idea behind CF is quite intuitive: if two users agreed in the past, they will likely agree again in the future. Instead of relying on explicit item attributes like content-based systems, CF systems harness the power of user behavior, using ratings or purchase history to make recommendations.

Two core types of CF emerged: memory-based and model-based.

Memory-based CF, often referred to as neighborhood-based CF, uses the entire user-item database to generate predictions. It calculates the similarity between users or items, and predictions are made based on a weighted average of ratings of similar users or items.

Model-based CF, on the other hand, uses machine learning models to learn patterns from historical data, making it more capable of handling sparser data and accommodating larger scale problems. This category includes techniques like clustering, matrix factorization, and latent factor models.

4.2. The Magic of Hybrid Systems

Despite the apparent effectiveness of CF, it was not without its problems. Issues like first-rater problems, sparsity, and scalability proved challenging. As a result, researchers soon started looking at conglomerating attributes of both CF and content-based systems resulting in the emergence of Hybrid Recommender Systems.

In the early 2000s, various types of hybrid recommender systems were proposed. These systems attempted to combine the strengths of both CF and content-based systems while mitigating their weaknesses. For instance: content-boosted collaborative filtering, which utilized a content-based predictor to augment the collaborative data and alleviate the sparsity issue.

4.3. The Era of Deep Learning

More recently, recommender systems have begun to incorporate more complex machine learning techniques. The advent of deep learning models has created newer paradigms for recommendation technologies. Techniques like autoencoders, Convolutional Neural Networks (CNNs), and Recurrent Neural Networks (RNNs) provide an ability to extract abstract features automatically, which leads to more accurate and contextual recommendations.

The use of reinforcements learning in particular holds great promise for recommender systems, potentially providing a solution to the exploration-exploitation dilemma witnessed in traditional methods.

4.4. The Future of Recommender Systems

The field of recommender systems continues to evolve at a feverish pace, driven by advancements in machine learning techniques, the availability of big data, and the ubiquitous demand for personalized content. With expanding realms like context-aware, cross-domain, multicriteria, group, and active learning recommender systems, the future promises to be an exhilarating ride of discovery and development.

The industry holds optimism that envisions recommender systems that not only accurately predict user preferences but also understand the underlying reasons behind those preferences, leading to a comprehensively personalized user experience. This historical journey through the evolution of recommender systems underlines the fact that there is yet a lot to uncover, improve, and enhance in this field. The world of recommender systems is full of potential, awaiting novel ideas and inventive minds to push the boundaries of what is possible even further.

Chapter 5. Synergy between Reinforced Learning and Recommender Systems

The inherent marriage between reinforced learning and recommender systems is nothing short of revolutionary, changing the ways we perceive and interact with digital mediums, while providing a viewing experience that seems almost tailored for each individual.

5.1. Foundations of Reinforced Learning

Before we uncover the synergy, a basic understanding of reinforced learning is important. Reinforced Learning, or RL, is a facet of machine learning where an agent learns to make decisions by interpreting its surroundings and receiving feedback. This takes the shape of rewards or punishments, pushing the agent to make decisions that maximize the received reward.

As an example, consider any video game. The ultimate goal may be to complete levels, but the agent - in this case, the player - undergoes multiple encounters that require continuous decision-making, like overcoming obstacles, defeating enemies, or collecting bonus items. The reward is consequently the progress made in the game; the more efficient the decisions, the more rewards are gathered, guiding the agent's learning.

5.2. RL in the Context of Recommender Systems

Recommender Systems have become an integral fixture in the world of online content delivery. Their primary job is to use a variety of algorithms to analyze user behavior and preferences to make accurate content recommendations. RL can significantly enhance this process as it instills the ability to adapt and learn continuously from user interactions.

Basically, a recommendation can be seen as an action made by the RL agent (the system) whose aim is to maximize the possible reward (user engagement). The reward can vary: a click, a like, a share, a purchase, and the system continues to reinforce actions that lead to positive feedback.

5.3. Combining RL with Traditional Methods

Reinforced learning, when applied to recommender systems, is often blended with more traditional methods like collaborative filtering, content filtering, or hybrid models to gain context.

For instance, collaborative filtering bases recommendations on users with similar characteristics, while content filtering suggests items similar to those that a user liked before. Reinforced Learning brings another dimension where the system dynamically adapts to user behavior changes over time.

5.4. Case Study: RL-Driven Recommendation at Youtube

Youtube is a classic example where RL has been exploited for content recommendations. Their recommendation algorithm uses a two-stage process: candidate generation and then ranking. They adopted RL to improve the second part: ranking.

In this phase, a handful of videos are sorted according to their probable watch time. This decision is based on both immediate engagement (like clicks) and long-term user satisfaction, such as reducing the number of times users hide recommendations from specific channels. Consequently, Youtube valued RL as it seeks for long-term reward maximization, which aligns with long-term user satisfaction.

5.5. Overcoming the Cold Start Problem with RL

The cold start problem is a classic issue in recommender systems where new users or new items pose a challenge, as there is no historical data to base recommendations on. RL can help solve this issue. Since reinforced learning thrives on experimenting with actions and learning from rewards, its trial-and-error based approach can be used to learn about new users or items and to generate recommendations accordingly.

5.6. Balancing Exploration and Exploitation

One crucial advantage of reinforcing learning in recommendation systems is the capability to balance exploration and exploitation. Exploitation involves selecting actions which are known to yield good rewards, while exploration refers to trying out less certain actions to discover potentially better rewards.

When the system suggests purely based on user history (exploitation), recommendations may be accurate but could lack diversity. On the other hand, purely exploratory recommendations can harm user satisfaction due to a lack of accuracy. RL can balance both, making sure the user gets accurate suggestions that also have an element of diversity and novelty.

In conclusion, the fusion of Reinforced Learning with Recommender Systems holds a tantalizing promise for the digital content space. It provides an avenue for continuously learning and adapting to user tastes while inherently handling diverse pains typical to the recommendation process. As these technologies are further refined and developed, the synergy between them will undoubtedly continue evolving, shaping our digital interactions in ways that feel incredibly personalized and intuitive.

Chapter 6. Data Requirements: The Fuel of Reinforced Learning

At its core, Reinforced Learning is a machine learning paradigm that relies heavily on the concept of learning from interaction. Consequently, the quality of this interaction — the data — forms the very basis of how successful this learning process can turn out to be. It's then easy to see why data, aptly dubbed the 'fuel' of reinforced learning, is the propellant that drives the entire learning machinery forward.

6.1. Understanding Data in Reinforced Learning

In the realm of Reinforced Learning, data is synonymous with experiences, and not just simple raw data points. An agent operates by interacting with its environment following a specific policy, gains experiences, and gradually refines its policy based on the feedback (reward) it receives. This constant cycle of action, observation, reward, and adaptation is crucial to reinforced learning.

However, the quality, quantity, diversity, and utility of these experiences (data) can greatly influence the learning outcome. Let's delve deeper into the intricacies.

6.2. Quality and Quantity: The Balancing Act

As with most areas of machine learning, quality and quantity of data play an instrumental role in reinforced learning. Quality data is the information that is truly representative of the object or scenario that you are looking to understand or predict. It's the data that doesn't consist of irrelevant noise and follows the real-world trends and patterns.

On the other hand, quantity is about having enough data to extract meaningful insights. The more data you have, the better your agent can learn from it, provided the data is representative of the states that the agent might encounter.

In Reinforced Learning, having a plethora of high-quality data allows the agent to explore its environment more comprehensively. It also ensures a better estimation of the value functions and the policy. Remember, though, more data can also mean more computational complexity and resource consumption.

6.3. Diversity: Encouraging Exploration

In addition to the quality and quantity, the diversity of data is crucial. Diverse data ensures the agent explores a wide range of scenarios, helping it to develop effective strategies for a broader spectrum of states. The role of diversity becomes more important when one considers that the objective of reinforced learning is the maximization of cumulative rewards over time, not just immediate feedback.

Therefore, encouraging active exploration of new states and actions (even those that might seem initially disadvantageous) can unveil powerful long-term strategies. This exploration-exploitation trade-off is central to many reinforced learning algorithms like epsilon-greedy, upper-confidence-bound (UCB), and Thompson Sampling.

6.4. Utility: Meaningful Data for Valuable Interactions

Utility refers to how meaningful and beneficial the data is for the learning process. Not all experiences are equally valuable; some might provide essential insights into achieving a high-reward state, while others may offer little to no value.

In Reinforced Learning, efficient algorithms prioritize experiences that are likely to provide valuable insights, commonly known as "Prioritized Experience Replay." This not only accelerates the learning process but also enhances the quality of the learned policy.

6.5. Real World Data Challenges

In real-world scenarios, data for reinforced learning comes with its own set of challenges. It's often not feasible for the learning agent to explore each possible state-action pair in the environment due to the massive state-action space. This is particularly true for real-world applications, such as robotics, autonomous vehicles, or finance, where it can also be risky or costly to make random explorations.

Meanwhile, data privacy and security concerns add another layer of complexity. When building content-based recommender systems, one should ensure that the user's private data is being handled with the highest standards of security and confidentiality.

6.6. Reinforced Learning in Content-Based Recommender Systems

In the context of content-based recommender systems, reinforced learning's data requirements become very specific. The system needs data on user behavior, preferences, feedback on recommended content, system engagement levels, and the attributes of the content itself.

All these data dimensions — quality, quantity, diversity, and utility — play a vital role and pose unique challenges in this space. High-quality data ensures reliable recommendations; abundant data enables understanding of both explicit and implicit user behavior; diverse data helps in covering a wide range of user preferences; and highly utilitarian data, those depicting clear user-system interactions, drive personalized content delivery.

At the end of the day, reinforced learning is a hungry machine powered by data. And the more high-quality, diverse, and useful that fuel is, the better and efficient the machine becomes. The exact data requirements might look different based on the specific use case, but these general principles will hold up against any application, shaping the future of reinforced learning systems.

Chapter 7. The Mechanics of Content Personalization

The digital age has wrought about a seismic shift in how we consume content. Creators can no longer uniformly disseminate content; instead, they must tailor it for layers of segmented audiences. The sophisticated systems that make this possible rely heavily on a novel concept in Machine Learning (ML) known as Reinforcement Learning (RL). This subset of ML enables a system to learn, adapt, and make optimal decisions through a system of rewards and punishments in a dynamic environment. With the integration of RL and Content-Based Recommender Systems (CBRS), it is possible to offer an individualized user experience.

7.1. Reinforcement Learning-Based Personalization

Reinforcement Learning (RL) is a significantly powerful tool in content personalization. The inherent architecture of RL allows for learning in a dynamic environment - it continually interacts with the environment or user, takes actions based on the current state, and then modifies the next steps according to the obtained results.

To illustrate, let's consider a video streaming platform. After a user watches a movie, the RL algorithm assesses the user's reaction. If the user immediately watches a similar movie, it is counted as a reward, and the algorithm learns that the user has a preference for that genre. On the contrary, if the user stops watching midway or skips to another genre, it is seen as a punishment, and the algorithm adjusts its recommendations.

At the core of RL lies the principle of maximizing total reward over the long run. The learning agent seeks to balance exploration (trying new, unvisited 'states' or content) and exploitation (opting for familiar content based on previous responses).

7.2. The role of Bandit Algorithms

One of the crucial aspects of RL is its utilization of bandit algorithms. These algorithms function in situations with a limited understanding of the user's preferences. They help in making a choice between known preferences and new opportunities, optimizing for the best outcome.

The concept of 'Multi-armed Bandit' provides a suitable analogy. It refers to a hypothetical gambler at a row of slot machines, each one providing a different, unknown reward distribution. The gambler must decide which machines to play, how many times to play each machine, and in what order to play to maximize his return.

Similarly, an RL-based recommendation system may have multiple content options (the arms of the bandit), with the goal of maximizing user engagement. The recommendation system must decide what new content to suggest and must continually adjust its strategy with each user-system interaction.

7.3. Data Selection and Feature Extraction

The success of a recommendation system largely depends on the quality of the data fed into them and how they process this data. Factors, or 'features,' that are usually considered include content attributes (for example, genre or author of a book), user history (previous interactions with similar content), and user behavior (time spent on particular content).

The system's ability to accurately extract features and learn from them significantly influence how effectively the system can predict user preferences. Content-based recommendation systems use these features to draw up a content user-profile. This profile serves as a 'digital reflection' of the user's preferences, which are continuously updated in real-time to align with evolving tastes and preferences.

7.4. Challenges in Implementing RL-based Personalization

Despite the promise of RL-based mechanisms, certain challenges may complicate their implementation. One primary concern is the trade-off between exploration and exploitation, commonly referred to as the exploration-exploitation dilemma. While it is essential for the system to gather new data (explore), it is equally important not to compromise the user experience by offering content that is radically different from the user's accustomed preference (exploitation).

The quality of recommendation also heavily depends on the 'Cold Start Problem,' where providing recommendations for new users with hardly any interaction history can be tricky. In absence of user history data, systems often resort to popularity-based recommendations, which lacks personalization.

Moreover, the privacy-security balance is a persistent concern in personalization algorithms. While information helps to personalize, over-reliance on personal data can infringe on privacy protocols. Balancing the need for data with respect for user privacy is an essential task for building ethical and functional personalization systems.

7.5. The Future of Personalization

The trailblazing progress of reinforcement learning and its application in content-based recommender systems is changing the face of personalization. As scientists push the boundaries of this exciting field, we expect more nuanced and effective systems to transform our digital experiences.

One promising area is the integration of natural language processing with recommendation systems, enhancing their predictive capabilities. Future systems could process human language, understand content, and provide personalized interactions, transforming how we engage with content.

Another thrilling prospect is the fusion of RL with Deep Learning (DL) techniques, forming a branch known as Deep Reinforcement Learning (DRL). These deep learning algorithms can learn complex patterns in data, providing richer profiles for user personalization.

These advancements promise to bridge the gap between machine understanding and human preference, striving for a future where human interactions with the digital world are as natural and intuitive as human-to-human interactions. On this technological journey, every step taken in RL research unfolds vast opportunities for content personalization. The next forte of ML, RL in content-based recommender systems, is teeming with potential, poised to redefine our digital experiences.

Chapter 8. Case Studies: Successful Applications of Reinforced Learning

The universe of artificial intelligence and machine learning is broad and diverse. But few strands of this complex web of technology capture imagination and practicality as brilliantly as Reinforced Learning (RL). In this chapter, we delved into actual, tangible, and transformative case studies that illuminate the powerful impacts of RL in various domains.

8.1. Ghostly Assistants: Reinforcement Learning in Gaming

Remember the spooky, deterministic ghosts in Pac-Man that seemed hell-bent on ending your game prematurely? Google's DeepMind developed a technique to leverage RL to train smarter ghosts, making more challenging adversaries for Pac-Man. The RL agent learns from trial and error, exploring the game mechanics, understanding the optimal measures, and improving ghost behavior - all in real-time. Game designers can harness these algorithms to create immersive and dynamic gaming experiences that respond and adapt based on player behavior.

8.2. Street-Smart Intelligence: Reinforcement Learning in Autonomous Vehicles

Applications of RL aren't just virtual; they manifest wonderfully in the physical world too. Autonomous vehicles offer a stunning example. Companies like Waymo and Tesla are incorporating RL algorithms to navigate complex, unpredictable, real-world environments. Here, the RL agent learns optimal driving policies by interacting directly with the environment — traffic, roads, obstacles — and receives rewards for safe, efficient driving. This ongoing learning and adaptation promise an exciting future where self-driven cars are responsive, safe, and resilient.

8.3. Engaging Grooves: Reinforcement Learning in Music Recommendation

Music recommendation systems represent yet another remarkable application of RL. Spotify's Discover Weekly and Daily Mix playlist recommendations have won many hearts with uncanny accuracy and intuition. This is all thanks to the RL algorithms behind the scenes. The RL agent rewards engagement (song plays, song completion, additions to playlists) and takes into account the many nuances (listening time, song order, skipped songs, etc.). The agent gradually builds an understanding of a user's musical taste, and in turn, suggests songs that align with these preferences.

8.4. Trading Profits: Reinforcement Learning in Financial Systems

In the volatile world of stock trading, RL is proving to be an invaluable ally. Financial institutions are exploring RL algorithms to predict and optimize trading decisions. The RL agents learn successful trading strategies, informed by historical data, and adapt to changing market conditions to maximize returns and mitigate risks. Algorithms trained with RL offer a tool to investors for systematic, disciplined, and emotion-free trading, transforming the financial landscape.

8.5. Personalized Entertainments: Reinforcement Learning in Streaming Services

Netflix and YouTube have changed the entire landscape of content consumption. One reason for their success is the precise, personalized recommendations they offer to users. This is made possible by RL algorithms in their recommender systems. Similar to Spotify's music recommendation, RL agents reward engagement (plays, likes, shares, comments, watch time) and continually improve the accuracy of recommendations, ensuring users always discover content they enjoy.

8.6. Enhanced Cybersecurity: Reinforcement Learning in Defensive Systems

In the ongoing battle against cyber threats, RL algorithms stand as the bold vanguard. Companies like Deep Instinct are deploying RL to anticipate and respond to new threats rapidly. Their RL algorithms learn from historical attack patterns and morph in response to new threats, improving system resiliency and reducing the window of vulnerability.

The highlights above are just glimpses of the grand realm of possibilities RL provides. With ongoing research and the expansion of RL algorithms across industries, the day isn't far when our digital and physical realities will be fundamentally shaped, enhanced, and personalized by reinforcement learning. While the challenges are still many, from the need for vast amounts of data to the complexities of real-world environments, the potential rewards promise an exciting future.

Chapter 9. Challenges and Ethical Considerations in Utilizing Reinforced Learning

Reinforced learning (RL), a subset of Machine Learning, is a self-evolving learning method where evaluation and reward mechanisms are utilized to attain optimal results. This type of learning incorporates trial and error sequences to determine the best action for a given situation. Despite its innovative application scope, challenges arise when applying RL, along with an array of ethical considerations.

9.1. Overcoming the Challenges in the Application of RL

Broadly speaking, RL strategies face four primary challenges: the lack of efficient exploration methods, instability, and variability of learning, the requirement of reward engineering, and the rare but catastrophic failures that can put systems at risk.

One of the main challenges involves identifying efficient exploration techniques. In RL, an agent must consistently shift between investigating and exploiting to maximize rewards. This constant change can lead to an exploration vs. exploitation tradeoff, where ensuring a balance becomes a challenge. Innovative exploration techniques, such as Upper Confidence Bound (UCB) and Epsilon-Greedy strategy, have made considerable strides towards addressing this issue. However, these methods are far from a concrete solution and involve meticulous examination in their application.

Next in line are the instability and variability of learning in RL, driven by the compounded effect of errors due to the iterative update process. In RL, the policy is continuously changing, thus making the data distribution non-stationary. This issue is commonly tackled by incorporating experience replay and target networks into learning strategy.

The third challenge is the requirement of meticulous reward engineering. Defining rewards is a significant challenge; if the rewards are too sparse, it becomes challenging for the agent to learn. On the other hand, if they are too densely packed, the agent may end up finding shortcut solutions that do not truly solve the problem at hand.

Lastly, one can encounter the rare but catastrophic failures in RL systems. They result from enhanced explorations, wherein agents can take up damaging actions to gain new experiences. These failures, though rare, can delay or even halt training entirely.

9.2. Ethical Quandaries in RL

When considering the ethical implications of RL, three key elements stand out: the inability to fully assure safety, lack of interpretability, and the potential for misaligned objectives.

In regards to safety, the challenge lies in assuring that the system will not take detrimental or harmful actions during its exploration phase. This becomes particularly critical when RL is applied to real-world systems, such as self-driving cars or medical algorithms.

In addition, the lack of interpretability of RL systems is a concern. Interpretability refers to the degree to which a human can consistently predict the model's result. Reinforcement learning algorithms, by nature, can become increasingly complex and opaque, leading to what is often termed as the "black box" phenomenon. As a result, tracing the decision-making process of these systems can be challenging.

The third ethical issue pertains to the potential for the misalignment of objectives between these systems and their human users. If the system's goals are not accurately aligned with those intended by the designers or users, this may result in unintended and possibly harmful outcomes. Tying this back to the issue of reward engineering, if the defined rewards do not accurately represent the end goal, the system may perform undesired actions.

9.3. Future Directions

Despite the aforementioned challenges and ethical considerations, RL's potential in numerous applications cannot be underestimated. To harness this potential, establishing regulations and ethical guidelines surrounding its use becomes crucial. Steps towards improving interpretability and exploring safe exploration techniques are also necessary.

In conclusion, reinforced learning comes with its shares of challenges and ethical questions. However, these difficulties do not deem it unfeasible. They merely illustrate the areas that need careful consideration, exploration, and discussion as we continue to advance in this domain. As we move towards a digital era where more decisions are entrusted to machines, the responsible design and deployment of RL are essential to ensuring a safe and ethical technological landscape.

Chapter 10. The Future: Emerging Trends and Opportunities

Firstly, it is critical to acknowledge that as we look ahead, the impact of reinforced learning and its application in content-based recommender systems is poised to revolutionize several industries. From e-commerce to entertainment, healthcare to customer service, reinforced learning algorithms are enabling unprecedented levels of personalization.

10.1. Reinforcing E-Commerce

In the realm of e-commerce, enhanced user experience reigns supreme. The more personalized, intuitive, and seamless the shopping experience, the higher the likelihood of converting prospects into regular customers. With the integration of reinforced learning algorithms, executing projects like customer segmentation, personalized advertisement delivery, and improved product discovery become a reality. The algorithm iteratively learns from the customer's online behaviors, preferences, and interactions, allowing for more accurate product recommendations, which in turn increase revenue, profitability, and customer satisfaction.

Moreover, these recommender systems hold substantial potential in inventory management, price optimization, and forecasting. Addressing these critical domains with reinforced learning can lead to dynamic pricing strategies, more accurate supply and demand prediction, and strategic replenishment approaches, all of which contribute to a smarter and more efficient e-commerce ecosystem.

10.2. Entertainment and Streaming Platforms

The burgeoning streaming sector, spanning music, videos, television shows, and podcasts, is increasingly benefitting from reinforced learning algorithms. As they parse through immense datasets of user preferences, watch histories, and search patterns, recommender systems progressively fine-tune their content delivery. Netflix's recommendation engine, Spotify's 'Discover Weekly', and YouTube's suggested videos are all emblematic of this growing trend.

Furthermore, with the augmentation of viewer-sensitive data like location, time, and device, these platforms can identify and predict the trending content among different demographics. Films, songs, or series that could otherwise sink into obscurity can find their way into the limelight, courtesy of such AI-supported systems.

10.3. Transcending into the Healthcare Sphere

Healthcare's digitization is another vital area where reinforced learning and content-based recommender systems could shine. With a focus on personalized healthcare, AI can break a trail in predictive analysis, patient monitoring, drug discovery, and treatment recommendation.

For instance, a reinforced learning algorithm can analyze historical and real-time patient data to derive critical insights about disease patterns, therapy responses, and likely risks. In conjunction with content-based recommendation systems, these insights then facilitate personalized treatment plans, recommend preventive measures, or suggest lifestyle amendments tailored to each individual's unique profile.

10.4. Customer Service Enhanced with AI

The customer service industry can also harness the strength of reinforced learning for chatbots, email assistants, and helpdesk bots. These AI-powered tools can learn from multiple customer interactions, enhancing their accuracy over time and providing increasingly personalized responses.

Their applicability extends beyond just immediate response. For instance, these bots could provide product recommendations based on query history or guide users through complex instructions, enhancing user interaction and satisfaction dramatically.

10.5. Progress and Prospects

The potential for reinforced learning usage is seemingly endless, cutting across various sectors that rely heavily on data and customer interaction. As AI progresses and dovetails with content-based recommender systems, new opportunities are bound to emerge.

Yet, it is essential to be mindful of the associated challenges. Data privacy concerns, maintaining the human touch in AI-driven systems, and the potential risks of over-personalization are all aspects that warrant careful attention. However, ensuring the balanced application of this technology can usher in an era of enhanced productivity, engagement, and satisfaction, heralding a future where human experience is authentically amplified by artificial intelligence.

Chapter 11. Final Thoughts: The Road Ahead for Reinforced Learning in Recommender Systems

Despite the lucidity already shed on the subject, a parting glance at its future possibilities seems only fitting. Reinforced Learning (RL) and Recommender Systems are two fields that, although standing tall on their own, mark a synergetic union of sorts in the context of this report. This amalgamation has undoubtedly spawned novelty in a variety of disciplines, right from commercial personalization to precision in clinical diagnosis and more. However, we are only scratching the surface – the road ahead is teeming with uncharted territories waiting to be explored.

11.1. The Potential of RL Based Recommender Systems

The promise of RL based recommender systems extends beyond the foreseeable horizon. Considering the exponential growth of data, we've stealthily moved from a data-deficient to a data-saturated world in a matter of a few decades. Finding meaningful nuggets of information from this constant data deluge is challenging and granted, information filtering techniques have surely improved, but with RL based recommender systems, we can now navigate the data landscape with greater efficiency and personalization.

Customization is the key here. Offering the right recommendation at the optimal time is an art that involves intricate user behavior modeling which RL systems effectively tackle. But the systems to come can take this forward by evolving into proactively intelligent units that would also consider the emotional and situational context of a user.

11.2. Tackling Technical Challenges

Undeniably, the journey to this promising future isn't without obstacles, many of which are technical in nature. One of the common issues plagues the area of exploration-exploitation trade-off. This balance is crucial to ensure that the algorithm explores unknown possibilities for improved recommendations while effectively utilizing known user patterns for instant satisfaction. Advanced methods such as Upper Confidence Bound (UCB) and Epsilon-Greedy policies are being studied to strike this balance.

Data privacy, a construct that will only gain importance in the future, is another challenge. RL based engines must be robust to accommodate privacy regulations without compromising on the customization degrees of recommendations.

Increasing the interpretability of models is also on the to-do list. While a recommender system may provide an apt suggestion, the lack of justification can be off-putting. Future models should be more transparent and explainable, offering users insight into how conclusions were reached thereby increasing user trust.

11.3. Next-Gen RL Algorithms and Models

Novel RL models and architectures that can better assimilate and act upon input data are in development as we speak. Deep Reinforcement Learning (DRL) is a testament to this. It marries the best of RL & Deep Learning (DL) to create models that are capable of extracting structure from raw data to make intelligent decisions.

Hybrid systems are another trend brewing in the labs of AI

researchers. These systems take a multi-pronged approach, incorporating collaborative and content-based filtering along with RL to generate recommendations. These hybrid systems aim to offset the limitations of individual methods and provide a more nuanced and comprehensive recommendation pool.

11.4. A Shift Towards User-Centric Approach

While we arm ourselves with advanced technologies, it's important to not lose sight of the fact that at the end of the day, it's about the user. As we move forward in time, an elevated focus on user-centricity is imminent. This means building recommender systems that are tailored not just based on observed behaviors but also capturing unexpressed needs and wants - essentially a shift from 'observed behavior' to 'latent needs'.

11.5. Conclusion

In sum, the road ahead for RL in recommender systems is filled with exciting challenges and alluring promises. It starts with overcoming technical hurdles like the exploration-exploitation trade-off, interpretability, and data privacy. Simultaneously, the development of next-generation RL algorithms and hybrid models is set to play a pivoting role in its development.

The final destination, however, is to cater to the user, to fulfil their tacit needs and provide a seamless, intuitive, and enriching digital experience. This journey of continuous evolution and adaptation is emblematic of the broader narrative of technological evolution. It anticipates a future where machines are not just tools, but partners in shaping better human experiences. The road is long and winding, but with every step, we come closer to untangling a part of the complex tapestry that is human behavior, preferences, and needs.

Not merely an end in itself, each stride forward in the realm of RL in recommender systems is a step towards a more personalized and efficient digital world.